Hearing From God

The magazine, *Prophecy Today,* which seeks to bring the unchanging word of God to a changing world is available on personal subscription as well as from Christian Bookshops.

A bi-monthly update audio-tape is also produced, providing a biblical perspective on current world events.

Further details of these and other PWM publications, including details of *The Centre for Biblical and Hebraic Studies* are available from the address below.

Published by PWM Trust, Registered Charity Number: 326533

The Park, Moggerhanger, Bedford, MK44 3RW, UK
Tel: 01767 641400 Fax: 01767 641515
Email: pwm@the-park.u-net.com

© 1999 PWM Trust

ISBN 1 872395 50 3

Typeset by Andrew Lewis, PWM Trust
Cover photo: PA
Printed by: Print By Design, Bawtry, Doncaster

Introduction

'Take a scroll and write on it all the words I have spoken to you' (Jeremiah 36: 2).

Since 1985 the magazine *Prophecy Today* has been publishing articles and reports on a wide variety of contemporary issues. The overriding objective in everything published has been to enable the people of God to discern what God is saying to his people today. The method of discernment used has been drawn from biblical principles, basically using the same criteria as was used by the prophets and is found in the teaching of Jesus and the apostles.

The prophets of Israel believed that the word of God could be discerned as much from what they called 'the deeds of the Lord' as from hearing him speak to them. Often the two were linked; the prophets would see something happen, or hear of a reported event, and God would speak to them concerning its significance.

The Bible declares that the nature of God is unchanging – he is the same yesterday, today and for ever. It was on the basis of this consistency, in contrast to the capricious nature of the Baals, that the prophets were able to declare the word of God with confidence. Elijah, for example, knew that God could answer him on Mount Carmel, whereas the gods of the false prophets were powerless to heed the cries of their devotees (1 Kings 18).

If we deny that God is able to communicate with us today we deny the unchanging nature of God.

The prophets also believed in the sovereignty of God that, in the words of Isaiah, he held the nations in his hands as 'a drop in a bucket' (Isaiah 40: 15). They continually warned that his good purposes for the nations could be frustrated by the disobedience of the people. It was for this reason that God, in every generation, pleaded with his people to listen. The major complaint brought by Jeremiah throughout his long ministry was that neither the leaders nor the people listened to the word of the Lord. The consequences of their stubborn refusal to listen eventually became inevitable. Jeremiah lived to see the terrible fulfilment of the tragedy he had prophesied – the destruction of Jerusalem and the slaughter of her citizens.

In times of crisis God always raises up prophets to speak to the people. It is not his desire that suffering and disaster should come upon anyone. He therefore sends warnings in the hope that there will be repentance and turning away from the ways that lead to destruction. The whole history of Israel is interspersed with such prophetic warnings, drawing attention to the consequences of policies being followed by the leaders of the nation, or by the moral behaviour and spiritual condition of the people.

In the New Testament prophetic warnings were given of famine, of persecution from the authorities, of economic hardtimes as well as warnings about the consequences of immoral behaviour, idolatry and becoming contaminated with the values of the world.

In the closing decades of the twentieth century prophecy became a regular feature of life in churches of many different denominations throughout the world. This is in contrast to the many centuries when prophecy was almost unknown following its forcible suppression by the church of Rome in the fifth century. A distinctive feature of modern prophecy is that it comes, not simply from well-known individual prophets, but from ordinary believers. Churches throughout the world have members who are learning to listen to God and are sharing with others the things they are hearing.

Inevitably there have been problems with false prophecy, especially where these have been of a predictive nature and have been given by well-known leaders and widely circulated. The problem has been compounded by the lack of teaching in the church concerning prophecy and as a consequence of its neglect over many centuries. There have, therefore, been no recognised set of criteria for handling revelation.

In New Testament times, and in the Early Church, prophecy was a regular feature of congregational life. There was, however, a recognised distinction between those who were called to the 'ministry of the prophet' and those who exercised the 'gift of prophecy'. The former were usually found in itinerant ministries such as that of Agabus who travelled around the congregations of Judea. By contrast, the gift of prophecy was exercised within the local congregation by ordinary church members who came under the discipline of their elders for the exercise of spiritual gifts.

The Didache records the regular practice of testing prophecy and lays down a number of rules that were followed in the Early Church. Clearly they recognised the truth of Paul's statement in I Corinthians 13 that 'we prophecy in part' (v 9). In other words, the words spoken in the church were a mixture of human origin and divine revelation. All such words had to be carefully weighed and tested. Paul warned the Thessalonian church that prophecies should not be treated with contempt, but the members were strictly instructed to 'test everything. Hold on to the good. Avoid every kind of evil' (1 Thessalonians 5: 19–22).

It is with this teaching in mind that the following collection of prophecies is offered.

Introduction

In publishing this collection of prophecies it should be emphasised that as a Ministry Team we do not believe that modern prophecy is on a par with scripture. Indeed, the Bible not only contains all that is needed for the full and final revelation of the word of God, it is also the plumbline of truth by which we judge anything thought to come from God today.

We do believe that God communicates with us today through the ministry of the Holy Spirit, but that does not mean that what we receive is word for word from the mouth of God. The Holy Spirit enables us to know what is on the heart of the Father and we express this in our human words.

Each one of these prophecies has been carefully weighed by the PWM Ministry Team who believe that they are trustworthy words. Each of them has been published in the magazine *Prophecy Today* over a period of fifteen years. Many of them refer to events that have already taken place and where the word has been fulfilled. They are of great interest, showing the progression of what has been received over a significant period of rapid change in world history. They have been received from many different people – some well-known leaders, others ordinary church members – all believers in the Lord Jesus, the Head of the Church who longs to give guidance to his people to enable them to fulfil the Great Commission, 'Go into all the world and make disciples of all nations ..... and surely I am with you always to the very end of the age' (Matthew 28: 19-20).

The prophecies are arranged in sections according to subject –

- **The Church**

- **The Church of England**

- **The British Nation**

- **International prophecies**

Within each section the prophecies are generally arranged in chronological order according to their date of origin. The source of each word is to be found in the notes at the end of the book. Wherever it has been necessary to add an editorial word of explanation or comment this is printed in italics.

Dr Clifford Hill
May 1999

Prophecies to the Church

All the prophecies in this section were directed towards the church as the people of God. They were not given for any specific congregation or denomination, but for believers in the Body of Christ

Sound the Trumpet

November 1984

My children, consider well your nation. Look around you, observe your homes, schools, business and institutions of law and government.

What do you see? Do you see the violence, the corruption, the rebellion and the anarchy? Do you see the anguish and suffering of the victims of such evil?

Do you see the anguish of your God? For I weep and grieve deeply over a nation that once honoured my name and respected my word; a nation that was once great, but is now grovelling in the dust. But I say to you even now, all is not lost.

Even though my righteousness demands that I severely judge the wickedness of this people, yet in mercy I wait. I wait for my people to come before me with weeping, fasting and prayer. I wait for intercessors who will continue to stand in the gap and hold back my hand of judgment, so I can continue to pour out my Spirit on this land.

But I warn you, in great earnestness, that I will not wait much longer. For although my Spirit is even now moving in great power through this land, Satan is also active, deceiving and lulling my people into a false peace of complacency and security, causing them to sleep instead of being alert to watch, and pray.

So I would have you sound the trumpet; calling my people to earnest, continuous prayer, so that I can fulfil my desire to pour blessings on this nation, rather than judgments.

Then once more, it will be said of this land; 'Blessed is the nation whose God is the Lord.'
[1]

If My People

May 1985

Thus says the Lord to the Christians of the West. 'I am longing to bring revival to you. I am longing to save the nations of the West whom I love. But the forces of corruption are already far advanced. They are eating like a cancer into the bodies of the nations. They are draining the life from the body, sapping the power to resist the destructive forces of the enemy.

'There will be no revival among the nations of the West until my people turn to me in true repentance. If my people who are called by my name will heed my word and turn from their faithless ways and come weeping before me with tears of true repentance then I will hear their prayer, for I love them, and I will pour out my Spirit upon them and heal their lands.' [2]

The Way of the Cross

November 1985

This is what the Lord says; 'My people have turned away from the cross. You say, "Lord we want to know you, to love you and serve you. We want to receive your power, to enjoy your presence, to feel your love, to know your nearness, to have the comfort of your abiding loving kindness. But do not speak to us of the cross. It is too hard for us.

We are but flesh and blood. We are weak and helpless children in a hostile world. Do not speak to us of persecution. Send us your power O God – power to resist the enemy, power to overcome all opposition, power to heal our diseases, power to witness for you. But do not speak of suffering or we will turn away. That way is too hard, Lord. It is too hard for us."'

'But it is MY way. It is the way I chose. It is the path I trod, It is the way of salvation of your God for his people. Is it too hard a thing for you to follow the way of him you call Lord and Master?

'Have you not heard? Have you not seen, that the everlasting God who neither slumbers nor sleeps, who holds the universe in his hands is calling you to fulfil his purposes? You pray, "Your kingdom come, your will be done on earth as it is in heaven". Do you really mean that or are they merely words?

The choice is yours. Follow your own way – the way of the world – that leads to death. Or follow my way, the way of the cross that leads to life eternal.' [3]

Tears of Joy

January 1986

There are tears of joy in the lives of many, and these tears are like precious jewels as they cascade in a glitter of joyous light. Like fresh dewdrops cradled in green leaves in the early dawn, so the tears of joy and fulfilment in the eyes of my children are a precious witness to my joy and delight in them, and their great joy and delight in me.

The tears of many sorrows are precious to me, too; these are the tears I will wipe away, and when all sorrow is gone, the jewel-like tears of joy will take their place. My children, you are in the world to help me with the tears of sorrow and anguish; it is your task for me, to take my love and compassion and the balm of my presence to overcome the sorrows and troubles all around you.

The tears of joy I will count and keep as a treasure to open to you at the time of fulfilment, when with joy and gladness and praise and singing you will meet round my throne with me and with all the children I have called by name. The crystal drops of tears of joy are the only tears known in heaven. The tears of the penitent will be wiped away, the tears of sorrow and pain and grief will be gently dried; and when all the tears of desperation and anguish and frustration have gone, I will bring forth in all their beauty and glory the tears of joy.

Only the tears of joy can make you beautiful, because they are the only beautiful tears. They dance and sing and sparkle as they fall, and they catch the colours of the sunlight in a joyous abandonment of rainbow colours, such colours as you cannot even dream of. There will be an enchantment of colour and light and love, and you will be filled with a divine joy and happiness in my unveiled presence.

There is laughter in heaven, my children, and you will be filled with a heavenly mirth, because your joy in me will know no bounds and restrictions. In this Valley of Shadow you have a glimpse of all this, but then you will know, and your joy in me will be complete. No, you don't understand why, in the world you know, there can't be more of the joy and happiness I have promised. Your own pride and wilfulness is the answer; even when you know and grasp the reality of me, you quickly let it go again.

You are beginning to learn and share and to reach up towards me, and I am giving you this and other words from me to share and encourage you all. Your way in this world is not an easy one, but as you are prepared to trust more and more in me and my leading, so I will give you increasingly a vision of the world I am preparing you for.

My dear children (and you are my dear children), gather close together with each other round me. I am gathering you closer and closer in my arms of love, that you may receive from me through each other the peace and strength and courage required of you to live my life in this world. You are, for me, the arms of love for others; I give so much in abundance to you, that it might be shared. In the sharing you will receive more and more until your whole lives reflect my glory and compassion. Yes, you will fail me, but you will never leave me, as I will never let you go.

Your tears of joy are precious jewels to me, and I am keeping them safe for you, as you go about doing my work in the place where I have called you to be. The many tears of life in this world surround you; all are transitory, only the tears of joy are from everlasting to everlasting. [4]

Receive from my Hand ...

March 1986

'Give me back my church. I have ordained it and brought it into being, and through it I will reveal my heart, declare my word and demonstrate my grace and power. For a long time I have patiently observed your ministry. Now I call you to witness MY ministry with wonder and joy in your hearts, for I am a living God who lives to demonstrate his nature towards all that he has created. Repent of dead works and outdated structures, and with confidence look to me to receive what I want to give in lavish abundance.

'Give me time and room to fulfil what I desire to do among you so that you will be relevant to meet the deep needs of a divided and disorientated world. My heart yearns over the world which I love so dearly, but my heart breaks over the complacency which I observe among my own people.

'Receive the warmth, reality and creativity of my love again so that with confidence and without fear you can walk into the future days of claiming the ground which belongs to you. This is a day for unity and not for division. It is a time for receiving from my hand rather than bewailing impotence and irrelevance. Agreement will not always be your lot, but the love which flows from the cross and is made real by my Spirit in the hearts of men will bind you in lasting fellowship.' [5]

A Word of Warning

January 1986

The times are urgent, my children, and you are not sufficiently aware of the pressing need calling for repentance and speaking into situations in the power of the Holy Spirit to proclaim my name. The Spirit of Antichrist is moving among the nations and is in your nation.

Unless you repent, all that is from the past will happen again but with severer form and yet more horror. This is because my people will not listen nor will they discern the times.

Seek my face, seek my Spirit and know that I would give you words to utter but you must pay the cost of commitment out of love. Trust me for I will enable you to do all things that I require so that my judgments may be turned just as they were at Nineveh when the king and the people repented at the preaching of Jonah. [6]

Times of Refreshing

March 1986

God is saying to us, 'I desire to restrain the darkness so that even though there is much shaking, nevertheless it will remain possible for my people to do the works of God and to bring in a great harvest through evangelism. I want my people to pray that I will restrain the darkness for this purpose. I desire to extend the time of grace during which it remains light, and in mercy to limit the shaking to that which will accomplish my purpose of causing men to despair of themselves and to turn to me for salvation.

'If my people will pray in this way, and if they are willing to repent and to do the works of God wholeheartedly while it remains possible to do so, then I will indeed restrain the darkness and maintain the conditions of light in which my work can be done.

'Cry to me to maintain the light, cry to me to send labourers into the harvest, and consecrate yourselves to be a holy people to carry out the Great Commission of evangelism in this lost world. If you will do this, then I will hear from heaven and send times of refreshing to you, for I desire revival rather than judgment.

'What I will do depends on the response of my own people, who are called by my name. If you will hear my call, then surely I also will be faithful to respond in this way; but if your ears remain closed, then surely I will allow the times of darkness to come upon you quickly. This is the hour of decision and I place the choice before you.' [7]

Follow Me

October 1986

Glittering lights of a pagan world
(Like dancing stars its pleasures twirled)
And all its billowing greed unfurled;
Do you love me more than these?

A world where self is plain to see,
Doing less for a larger fee,
Desiring gain and despising me;
Do you love me more than these?

Instead of seeking my Father's will,
They yearn for pleasures greater still,
And who cares if they cause others ill?
Do you love me more than these?

Societies steeped in idolatry,
From 'Easter' eggs to the 'Christmas' tree.
Their ways seem good ... but they overlook me.
Do you love me more than these?

Daughter of Babylon racing on
Unheeding till your doom shall come;
Think now, before all your hope is gone.
If you love me more than these, then ... FOLLOW ME!

I cannot promise you riches great,
In a world I shall terminate;
But when I come, through all eternity,
You can live and reign with me,
If you love me more than these
And FOLLOW ME ... NOW. [8]

Repentance and Revival

March 1988

On Saturday 5 March 1988 approximately two thousand Christians from all over the South of England converged on Westminster Central Hall for the National Call to Prayer and Repentance. At the same time, throughout Scotland, England, Wales and N. Ireland, approximately five hundred similar meetings took place, and hundreds of small meetings all offering up the same heartfelt prayer for the nation – 'Lord have mercy on us'. Approximately fifty thousand people are known to have taken part in the day of prayer.

In the Central Hall Westminster, the following word was received:

You have come before me today representing my church. I reaffirm my love and acceptance of you, that I have called and chosen you and will not discard you. As you come before me I cry to you, 'What have you done with my Spirit?' Did you not know what I wanted to do with my Spirit?

I have been sending my Spirit amongst you many years for holiness – but you continue to sin; to lead you into repentance – but you have chosen to substitute renewal – to witness but you have settled for entertainment.

How can it be that I would send my Spirit amongst you and you would so fly in the face of all he wanted and you would turn to your own ways? You have been putting me to shame in the world. I wanted repentance and revival and to touch a lost world for whom my heart aches.

You have taken my Holy Spirit and you have not allowed him to do what he wanted to do. Repent of these things and supplicate for the many brothers who do not know what they have done. You have made me grieve and made me weep. Will you not now repent and turn to the ways which I chose for you? [9]

The King is Calling

May 1988

How long must I bear your sin and iniquity?
How long must I bear your faithless ways?
How long will you pursue other loves
And spurn the one who gave you life?

When you were dead in your trespass and sin
I had compassion, I raised you up
From the depths of the pit to the height of the throne
My sons and daughters you have become.

And yet my love you have not returned
You took my gifts but rejected me
The riches of the world you preferred
More than the treasures of my house.

My covenant I have kept with you
Yet you have broken faith with me
My love for you will never change
O my people, come back to me.

If you repent with contrite hearts
I will receive you with gladness and joy
My holiness will be your crown
My righteousness your wedding gown.

You will see the glory of my face
Sit with me upon my throne
Be joined together in union of love
My Father's dwelling place become. [10]

Church Responsible for the Nation

<u>March 1988</u>

This is what the Lord is saying to his church in Britain: 'You are part of a nation that is under judgment. Yes, judgment has already begun. You have been receiving warnings for many years that you will never get the economy right or the social life of the nation onto a stable footing until you establish righteousness in the land. All these warnings have been ignored. But you have not been faithful in declaring the word of God during a time of rapid social change. It is for this reason that the enemies of the gospel have had such liberty to change the laws of the land and the media has displayed filthy language, lewd behaviour and made light of adultery and homosexual acts.

'All kinds of evil behaviour have been presented as the norm before the eyes of the nation. This is why family life is disintegrating, husbands and fathers desert their wives and children, wives desert their husbands and commit adultery with married or unmarried men, and young people fornicate with any who take their fancy of either sex.

'The nation is sick and heading for massive disaster, but I hold my church primarily responsible for the moral and spiritual life of this nation. You are the watchmen of the nation and you have not been faithful upon the walls of the cities to discern the onslaught of the enemy or to blow the trumpet to warn the people of danger, so the enemy has been allowed to come in like a flood and pervade the land.

'The land has been polluted by the shedding of innocent blood, by violence and pornography, by adultery and sodomy, by corruption and injustice, by greed and avarice, by oppression and unrighteousness, by lies and deceit, by witchcraft and idolatry and by a lack of compassion for the poor and the powerless.

'In the face of all this evil and corruption my voice is still not heard in the nation. The prophetic declaration of the word of God is not heard upon the lips of the leaders of the church. It is for this reason that the church languishes, its numbers are in decline, its finances are unhealthy and there is disunity, discord and a lack of vision.

'Now is the time to repent. Now is the time to recognise your faithlessness and the way you have strayed from the paths of righteousness and failed to uphold my word in the nation. If you will now repent publicly of your own sinfulness and declare my word within the church and in the sight of the whole nation, the people will respond. If you refuse to hear this word and harden your hearts against me, you will bring upon yourselves terrible consequences as the days darken across the nations.

'A great disaster is coming soon upon the nations which will engulf the people, and in the midst of it persecution will come upon the church. Remember that judgment begins at the household of God. The judgment you are now experiencing is mild by comparison with what will befall you in the days to come. You will cry out to me, but I will not answer, because when I cried out to you, you did not listen or pay attention to my word.

'Test me,' says the Lord, 'try me and see if I will not open the windows of heaven and pour out such a blessing upon you that you will not be able to contain, that will spill over into the life of the community around you and transform the life of the nation.

'How I long to pour blessing upon you. It is for salvation that I sent my Son, not for judgment, but to bring redemption to the world – that none might perish but that all might come to a knowledge of the one true and living God. That is still the desire of my heart and my purpose, for my plans are for good, not for evil. They and they only can give you a future and a hope. My message is still, "Turn to me and be saved all you nations of the world, for there is no other way of salvation."

'But that word is primarily addressed to the church as those who are sent to declare my word unto the nations. I hold each part of the body accountable for the nation unto whom you are called to witness in my Name and to declare my word.' [11]

Repent and Return

May 1989

'You have wilfully chosen to turn your back upon me, to neglect and reject my word and to substitute your own intellect, philosophies and desires. You have chosen to worship your own "gods" and to look within yourselves for the solutions to your problems.

'You have neglected to teach your children my truth and you have handed them over to darkness and confusion. In your selfishness and lust you have destroyed that which I have created and you have polluted the land with the blood of your unborn children.

'I am taking my hands of protection from you, and you will be overtaken by your own wickedness unless you repent and return to me. Even now you are seeing the effect of my anger and my lack of protection.

You have made yourselves "gods" taking into your own hands that which rightly belongs to me, the matters of life and death, of creation and destiny. But in my great mercy and because I still desire your good and not your destruction, I am shaking you to show that you are not the masters of your own destiny.

'Come to me and walk in my ways and I will restore you. But if you do not heed what I say then I will hand you over to the darkness you seek and to the rule of the "gods" you have chosen to worship.' [12]

Humble Yourselves

May 1989

Truly, says the Lord, in these days I am seeking those who are humble and contrite in heart and who tremble at my word. Those who despise my word I will treat with contempt, and those who will not humble themselves before me I will cause to be humbled in the sight of men.

Why is it that those who lead my people will do anything except admit their own helplessness? Those things for which they have longed, I have not done. I have not done them because they desired to build their own kingdoms and to receive the adulation of men, and not to build a kingdom for me and to give the glory where it is rightly due.

I have said that I will forgive and bring healing if my people will humble themselves and pray and seek my face and turn away from their wicked ways. Why then is it that those who lead my people are willing to pray, but not to humble themselves? They are willing to seek my face, but not to repent. It is because the prayer and the seeking of my face can be done in a state of pride, but humbling oneself and repentance requires a death-blow to pride.

I look upon the hearts of those who lead my people and I see pride and arrogance, I see the desire for self-glorification and I see an unwillingness to bow the knee before me and to admit their helplessness. They will turn to any channel which seems to offer a means of achieving what they desire.

I see those who have wanted the desires of my heart turning to those who have walked in deception. This grieves me, says the Lord. My heart is burdened, for if they do not turn back they will all fall together, deceived and deceivers alike. I am grieved at what is happening among the leaders of my people. I am grieved at the stubborn refusal to acknowledge that only God can achieve what needs to be achieved; there is no wisdom and no scheme of man which can accomplish it in place of the working of the Spirit of God.

Until there is a full acknowledgement that no might nor power can accomplish these things but the moving of the Spirit of God alone, I will wait for a people who will come before me in humility and lowliness of spirit, who will acknowledge that my word is true in every part, and know that I will not depart from one word of it.

I am looking for a people who will glorify me because I am God and not because they want to persuade me to release my power into their hands. I will not give them this power, declares the Lord, until there is humility before the throne of God, and repentance of pride and self-seeking. When my people admit that of themselves they can do nothing, then the hand of God will begin to accomplish those things which they cannot do in their own strength. [13]

When will you put Me First?

July 1989

When will my people put me first as the focus of their attention? Why do my people always long to rush forth and do great things for me, rather than seek me first and wait for my word of command? Why is it that my people long to rush forth to save unbelievers when I am calling them to seek me?

For so many years my people have neither sought me nor have they reached out to the unsaved world. Yet now when I call them first to seek me and minister to me as I desire they immediately want to rush out to save the world. I am not calling my people at this time to minister to the world but I am calling them to return to me.

How can they speak to the world about a God whom they do not even know? How can you send them out to preach salvation to the lost if you have not first sent them into my presence chamber to draw close to me, and understand whose ambassadors they truly are?

My people are like a parched and barren wilderness with little life, and what there is is stunted and feeble. Who is going to be attracted to live in a wilderness? I want to pour out my Spirit on my people in a way they have not known so that the barren wilderness may bring forth the rose of great beauty, of such untarnished sweetness and savour that men cannot fail to be amazed at it.

I do not want my people to go forth into the world to offer the death that is in the churches now, but I want my people to come to me to have the gift of life fanned into flame within them. I have a perfect order in all that I do. I have said that I sent my Spirit to call my people away from dead works of the flesh and into repentance, and away from self-pleasing and into witness. The holiness and repentance must come first, and then I will empower my people for witness.

I will not speak to this generation through unclean lips or through the elaborate schemes of men, or through powerless and impoverished lives, but I will speak through a church that has learned to draw close to me and to know me and to walk in the ways of my Spirit.

Minister first to me, attend first to my interests so that my bride may become what she should be; and then through her I will speak to the world. Reconsecrate my altar in the temple made of living stones. The hearts of my people are the altar and I desire to receive acceptable sacrifices from a purified altar. [14]

Love and Preferment

<u>November 1990</u>

The eyes of the church are on men and not on God. When that happens, acceptance of one another is replaced by suspicion and interrogation. Until you can accept each other from the heart there will be friction, backbiting and jealousy. Preach the message of reconciliation – one to one as well as one to God. Authority is not diminished by understanding and acceptance.

In the world of men and animals, acceptance is earned by ability and prowess. It must not be so with you. A genuine, humble preferring of each other is all that is desired, an exaltation of one another that can draw out and release the best from each other. That is more important than haranguing; within the framework of acceptance the principles of the Kingdom can be safely taught.

Fear must have no place, for fear builds walls, increases suspicion, brings mistrust and, ultimately, paralysis. Where there is true love there is no fear.

Look around and see. Who are the men, the women you admire the most? Are they not the ones who have been schooled in love? For many parade their gifts and attract much praise from men, but those whom I respect are those who make way for others out of love.

No longer is it sufficient to be right. The way in which you express the truth is as important as the cause itself. That is why it was my will to justify my servant Job. It is not that he did not sin in his ways and words, but that those who sought his betterment did not do so in love. And so I worked as I did to justify my servant Job to teach the way of love.

Do not portray me as a stern, uncomprehending Father – the Muslims do that. Though my anger waxes hot against all sin within my holy place, yet mercy triumphs over judgment. Call upon me together for mercy – not just for yourselves but also for your land, for when you know me as the God of mercy then indeed you will know me better. [15]

New Life in Christ

July 1994

This is what the Lord says, 'You will never reach the hearts of this nation until you, my people, who are called by my name, repent, and repent publicly, before the whole nation for the sins you have committed.

'You say, "But Lord, in what way have we sinned? How have we offended you?"

'By denying my word. By defaming my name in the sight of the nation.

'You ask, "How have we denied and defamed your name?"

'By publicly declaring your doubts about the truth of my word and by undermining the belief and trust of believers who do not have the biblical scholarship or the ability to understand the complex theories and theological propositions you propound.

'You have given occasion to secularists and to those of other religions to rejoice and to trample upon the faith of faithful believers. You have caused the enemies of the gospel to triumph and thus you have brought dishonour to my name by identifying my church with the unbelievers.

'You have allowed adultery to be practised in my church, even among the priests and pastors. They have publicly sinned, but they have not been publicly rebuked. Many have been allowed to stay in pastoral office. Others have openly declared that they have been committing sins which are detestable in my sight, but they have not been rebuked; instead they have been approved by those in high office. This has caused confusion in the nation and a lowering of moral standards.

'People say, "If it is all right for the priests to commit sin, then it must be all right for us." It is as it was in the time of Jeremiah, when I said, "Among the prophets of Jerusalem I have seen something horrible: they commit adultery and live a lie. They strengthen the hands of evildoers, so that no-one turns from his wickedness" (23:14).

'There are many anomalies and contradictions given to the nation by those who are regarded as "the church". These cause great confusion. They bring the gospel into disrepute and bring dishonour to the name of Christ.

'When will you begin to see yourself as others see you – disunited, squabbling over who should be ordained, arguing over basic moral standards, unsure of the fundamentals of the faith, unrighteous in the handling of money, not practising what you preach, making pronouncements that sound political rather than prophetic because they do not carry the authority of the word of the living God?

'The world overlooks the faithful pastors, the humble preachers and the multitude of faithful believers who have not bowed the knee to idols or forsaken the Word of God for the enticements of Mammon and the temptations of the flesh. The people of the world do not want to see these faithful ones because they are a rebuke to them. They prefer to see those who are like them, whose sinful image gives them comfort and strengthens their evil hands.

'The world does not distinguish between the true church and the apostate church, between faithful believers and faithless unbelievers. Even among those in high places there are many faithful believers, but they are secret believers who are controlled and muzzled by the fear of man. That is why their hands hang limp and their hearts are downcast; they feel powerless and oppressed, lacking the liberty of the Spirit and the joy of the Lord.

Turn to me now in simple trust and allow the Holy Spirit to fill you with new life and power. [16]

Removing the Boundary Stones

April 1994

God is looking over the nation, seeing everything; this is his accusation:
'The leaders of the nation have removed my landmarks – my laws, therefore judgment has come to the nation and it will continue to come in greater severity.

'Many leaders in my own church have removed my landmarks – my laws, therefore I am shaking my church in severe judgment. Remember what I have written: 'Cursed are those who remove the landmarks.'[1]

'Calvary shows the depth of my anger against lawlessness; it was there that I removed the curse of the law from my people, but I did not remove their obligation to honour the law. I gave my laws to be safeguards, and a blessing.

'I look now for those who will restore the laws to a place of priority in their hearts, their homes, and their congregations.

'If I see a response in this way I may use you to save your nation from my total judgment. I offer you a hope, and a way of escape to see if you will obey my word and pray for your nation.' [17]

---

[1] 'Cursed are those who remove the boundary stones' NIV

Walking on Water

November 1994

A prophecy to leaders in the church

'In the days which are to come, that part of the church which will survive and prevail as overcomers will be that part which has learned to walk upon the waters, trusting only in me. There will be such storms that it will no longer be possible, as it were, to cross the waters by the ordinary means of using a boat, for the storms will be such that any boat will founder.

'The ways of traditional church organisation will not be adequate for the needs, because they will be too rigid and inflexible to withstand the wind and the waves, and those who have put their trust in them for their security will be like those who find themselves in a boat which is overwhelmed and doomed to sink.

'In those days only those who have learned to walk upon the waters will walk in safety. Do not put my people into rigid formal structures, for to do this is to put them into a boat which will seem adequate and comfortable while the waters are calm, but will later become a place of death for those whose only experience has been to get in and enjoy the ride.

'The structure of my church is not to be like a ship, a monolithic whole, a structure created by men. It is to be my body, a thing which is completely mobile and flexible, able to respond and adapt to the needs of the moment.

'A body will survive; but any structure created through the wisdom and efforts of man will prove to be like the ship which will sink in the time of trouble and pressure. Do not over-organise my people but teach them the ways of God; teach them the way of listening for the voice of my Spirit, and of spontaneous action in obedience to those promptings.

'Teach them not to rely upon men, or upon any form of organised structure, but teach them that each one must have his trust solely in me, the Head of the body, who alone has the wisdom to guide his people through the stormy waters.

'The days are coming when every item of your security which depends upon the ways of man and the structures of the world will be taken from you. No matter how hard you have laboured to build it up and no matter how much my people have asked me to bless it, it will all be like having placed your treasure in a bank which has suddenly closed its doors to you and will permit you no access.

'Teach my people, therefore, the way of walking on the water. Teach them in these days while the waters are yet calm to put their eyes upon me with a whole-hearted intensity, and to trust me implicitly in all matters, whether they seem great or small.

'As each member learns to recognise and obey the instructions of the Head, so all together will begin to be able to function as one body.

'This will never come about through human organisation, but only as they learn to walk continually under the direct leading of my Spirit. Your task is not to organise them but rather to teach them how to walk hand in hand with me.

'Consider what is written in my word and hold it close to your hearts.

'Thus it is written, "Cursed is the man who trusts in man and makes flesh his strength, whose heart departs from the Lord, for he shall be like a shrub in the desert, and shall not see when prosperity comes, but shall inhabit the parched places in the wilderness, in a salt land which is not inhabited.

'Blessed is the man who trusts in the Lord, and whose hope is the Lord, for he shall be like a tree planted by the waters, which spreads out its roots by the river and will not fear when heat comes, but its leaf will be green; and will not be anxious in the year of drought, nor will cease from yielding fruit."

'Let me teach you how to live and how to lead my people according to this word, in order that I may have a people who are able to walk upon the waters in the day of the storm.' [18]

A Call to Holiness

January 1995

'My heart is breaking over the church in this land today. She is so selfish, so compromised, so self-seeking, so complacent. How can I use such a church to bring about my purposes?

'Why will you not recognise your arrogance, why are you so unwilling to repent? You have forgotten who you are, the price that I paid to bring you to myself.

'I gave you my precious only Son, whom I loved from before the dawn of time, and I allowed him to bear all your sin and your suffering and your wickedness, yet you fail to realise the magnitude of this.

'The only hope for you is to turn to me again, to be willing for me to break your arrogance and pride. You must become Christ-centred, and must rid your lives of all that is not of him.

'This will be hard for you, for you have been duped into thinking that it is all right to compromise and to be so comfortable in your 'Christianity'.

'You have lived lives of ease and plenty, and you are ill-equipped to cope with what will come, because of this.

'Make yourselves ready, for there are stormy seas ahead for my people, and you need to be prepared.

'I have been merciful to you, my people, and I long for you to turn to me.' [19]

Grieving the Heart of God

January 1997

My church is like a child harlot,
I weep over her,
Not because I condemn her,
But because she sells herself to the world.

She does this not knowing
That if she turned to me
I would give her so much better and more,
Because she is of value to me.

She brings me her earnings
And expects me to be pleased with them,
Oh how I weep over her,
But there is yet hope.

I will not forsake her
Because I love her,
But I want to show her
What it means to be my bride.

How to say 'no' to the world,
How to say 'no' to prostituting herself,
For her lovers will only let her down,
They will turn on her, but I will not.

It is a hard lesson she has to learn,
I desire that she willingly co-operate with me,
Learning to look at me with an open heart and mind
Laying down her ways and understanding.

And then I will come alongside her,
I will show her the truth,
The life that I offer,
The real value that she could have in me.

She is of real worth to me,
I weep over her,
Who will tell her
What is on my heart?

I know of her ignorance and need,
Yes, I call my bride to repent,
To change her ways,
But not as she understands repentance.

I do this out of love for her,
The repentance that I desire
Is not a sentence or punishment for her to endure,
It is freedom and release that I offer.

Release for her to come off the streets,
To become the beautiful bride that she could be,
That she has a right to be.
Oh, that she wants all that I want for her!

She is like a street urchin,
Dirty, underfed, unhealthy, dressed in rags,
She won't stand before me and be ready for change.
She thinks I will chain her up on a leash.

All that I ask is that she comes before me,
That she stands in my presence
Ready and open to hear me,
She must lay down her preconceived ideas to do this.

Then she will walk the land
And people will stand in awe of her,
My beautiful bride.

They will want what she has,
And she will bring them to me.

But if my bride continues to reject me
In favour of her own ways and ways of the world
Then I will be forced to act in more drastic ways;
For her sake and for the spread of the gospel in this land.

I have many lost sheep that I weep over and want to bring into my pasture,
But even if I do have to discipline her
It will be out of my love for her,
It will be for her good, even if painful for a time.

See how much I love her,
See how much I want to do for her,
See how I weep over her ... [20]

One of the special features of these days is the way in which children all over the world are receiving the Gospel with joy and gladness. They have a unique simplicity and freshness of faith. This has led many to believe that this generation of children are special in the purposes of God. This may be confirmed by the fact that children seem to be the target of the enemy and the victims of abuse in so many lands.

A prophecy about children in the purposes of God is given on page 57 'Out of the Mouths of children'. The following three prophecies were given by children during a time of worship in a children's camp in Scotland. The first is from a 13 year-old and the second from a 14 year-old, the third from a 13 year old.

I Will Keep you Safe

March 1990

'My voice is like thunder: it rings out across the mountains, and when I speak no one can help from hearing me. I will pass judgment on this world. Beware in the last days of people who say they come to help you; they just want to take away what you have.

'Beware of people who say they are comforting you, but are saying that God does not really care; they are traps from the devil.

'No matter what happens I will keep you safe, but keep your faith very, very strong in me. Trust in me at all times. Don't worry about having good praise meetings – I like them but time is short and you have to be strong in God; you have to trust in me. Remember I am the Lord your God. I'm your guarantee of safety, but if you don't have good faith in me, I can't help you. Just keep close to me.' [21]

Consecrated Children

March 1990

'Go and make disciples of all nations. I will raise up people to go into the countries of the world where there are no Christians, where the gospel has never been preached. I am seeking a generation which is consecrated to me.

'The generation which is consecrated to me is the generation which will see me come again in glory. If the generation which today's children are in is not consecrated to me, I shall wait for the next generation and if they are consecrated to me, I will come back in glory. I will shake out of leadership selfish leaders, and instead of false preachers I shall raise up prophets.

There is going to be immense change in the world, and you must be prepared for the change. You must pray for boldness and courage to take the gospel into places like Albania, North Korea, and Yemen.

'Even in your towns, villages and cities there are people who do not know the full meaning of the gospel.

'I will give the power to you so that you can go and fulfil my commands: but before I give this power to you, you must be prepared. So I say to you, be consecrated to me and be prepared for my power and might.' [22]

Miracles and Prayer

January 1991

During the camp a 13 year old girl felt God was sharing his heart with her, saying,

'My people are crying out to me. They need help. Their system of government is pulling them apart. Who can I send? Who will rescue them? I looked at the church: they were proud, scared of getting their hands dirty. I try to talk to them, but they are too interested in money. I try to teach them, but they are cold.

'I asked again, "who can I send? Who will rescue my people?" Then I heard the most beautiful thing in the world: children were praying, and in their hearts they were saying "Send me, I want to go". I wept when I heard them; they are so precious to me. I will answer them because their hearts are soft. I will talk to them more than ever before, because I love them.

'I have been calling – it seems for ever – "Who will go, who can I send?" – and children have answered, so I will make them powerful. I will treat them with care. I will pour out my Spirit two-fold on them, so that what they ask for, I will double. They will perform miracles and their faith will be huge. The Lord has heard and granted the prayer of the children.' [23]

Prophecies to the Church of England

All the prophecies in this section were specifically directed to the Church of England.

This first prophecy was given at a one-day conference of clergy of the diocese of Southwark. It came in a time of prayer in Southwark Cathedral being led by the Bishop of Southwark, the Right Rev Ronald Bowlby

Divine Healing Needed

May 1984

Thus says the Lord to the Church of England. 'You are to me like a woman aborting the life of a child from her body. She cares so little for the precious gift of life that she longs only to rid herself of it.

'You have aborted my word. You care so little for the gift of life I have given you that you cast it out and rid yourself of it. You do not care for my word; you care only for yourself. My church is my body and into it I have given the precious gift of life, but you have made it a body of death. The life you should have given to the world you have scorned.

'Therefore I will spew you out of my mouth. Therefore I will cast you aside because you are not faithful to my word.

'I call upon you now to look to yourself and then turn to me and be healed. I only can heal you. Recognise what you have become. Your harlotry is abhorrent in my sight and I will hold you responsible for this nation.

'Turn to me and be saved, then my Spirit will be poured out upon the people. Then will I heal the nation and the land will receive my blessing. I love you and I do not wish to come upon you in judgment, but in overflowing love, says the Lord.' [24]

You have been Robbed of your Power

April 1988

This prophecy was given at a conference of clergy and leaders in the Church of England during the third National Evangelical Anglican Congress (NEAC 3). It was read to the conference during a time of prayer by the presiding Bishop

See, I am going to do a great thing. All power is mine. Heaven and earth are mine. I control all things – nothing is outside my power, for I am the Lord.

As the rain falls from heaven and waters the earth, giving life, refreshing and cleansing, so I am going to pour out my cleansing power on you my people, so that you may be prepared vessels to show my glory. For indeed you need cleansing, you have so disappointed me. I placed you as a light to the nations, I longed that you might shine like the stars, a sign of my glory.

Yet you have compromised yourselves, you have been willing to lie down with the snake, saying 'We will be safe in the den of the serpent' and so you have been robbed of your power. The serpent has stolen your power. You have become tarnished, as blind as those you were meant to save. You do not see the poor, you do not hear the cry of the unloved, you do not stand with the oppressed, you do not speak out against injustice, you side with the powerful, saying 'These will protect us'.

Now, my people, I demand that you turn from your ways of compromise. Open your eyes, lift up your heads, see what you have become and open your hearts to me afresh. Be sorrowful. Fast and pray. Seek me with all your heart, and I will purify you. For you are my bride, my beloved. I cannot abandon you. I will cleanse you. It will be painful for you – great pain, but this will be a blessing, and I will revive you and bless your land. [25]

A Time to Reap

November 1988

The following prophecy was given in Durham at a public meeting in St Nicholas Church, 'The Church in the Market', in the city centre. It was at the time when David Jenkins was Bishop of Durham and he was replacing evangelical clergy with those who were in accord with his own liberal theology. David Jenkins' consecration as bishop had taken place in York Minster which had been struck by lightening a few hours later.

This is what the Lord says to the believers in Durham:

'Do not be afraid of the fiery trial that is among you. You are in the eye of the storm and I will keep you in perfect peace if you keep your eyes upon me and hold fast to the faith in which you have been grounded. Remember the scripture that if anyone comes and preaches a gospel other than that given through the apostles, he will be eternally condemned.

'The storm you are experiencing will sweep through the churches, separating the wheat from the chaff and exposing unbelief wherever it is found until the church is cleansed and purified and made ready for the task facing her in these and coming days.

'Do not be disturbed by men coming among you who appear to care for the people and yet deny the faith, for I have allowed them to come into high prominence in the nation. I am using them as I used Cyrus to do my bidding, though he was a pagan king who did not know my name. It is my purpose to use them to expose the unbelief that has been in the church for many years.

'I am sitting like a refiner of silver over my church. I lit the flame under the furnace with the lightning strike on York Minster. My church is in the furnace like a precious metal being heated so that the impurities come to the top. I will continue to expose them and remove them as the refiner skims the dross from the surface until he can see his face perfectly reflected in the metal.

'Understand that I have not abandoned my church, neither have I relinquished control to faithless men. Be encouraged that I am at work among you and be strengthened in your faith. Hold fast to the faith that sets you free from the fear of men and know that I love you and will never leave you. You are mine; my beloved people. Stand firm in the faith and hold fast to the word of life and you will rejoice in the victory that is surely mine, for I am the Overcomer, the Alpha and Omega'. [26]

A Call to Repent

March 1998

The following prophecy was given in Westminster Central Hall, London during the day of Repentance and Prayer. One of the speakers removed his clerical collar and stock and ripped it apart. The sound was picked up by the microphone and amplified around the hall with striking effect. He then directed a word specifically to the Church of England

'This is what the Lord says, As this clerical collar has been removed and torn asunder, so I will remove you from your position in the life of this nation and tear you asunder unless you repent and return to me.

'I am against you, says the Lord, because you have misused your position of responsibility in the life of this nation. You have not faithfully proclaimed my word. You have misused my word, you have adulterated my word, you have prostituted my word. I am against you because you are unfaithful shepherds and I will remove you unless you turn in repentance to me and acknowledge your sinful ways.

'This is what the Lord says. It is no use saying, "We are the Church of England established by law in the land". Do you not know that I can raise up servants from the stones of the ground to bring my word to the nation? I am longing to bring my word, but it must be MY word, for there is no other word that can save this nation from disaster.

'I am pleading with you to repent before me. Then I will pour out my Spirit to cleanse you and heal your divisions. Then I will pour out my Spirit upon the nation to heal the land.' [27]

I Hold you Responsible

July 1989

During Sunday morning worship at St Mark's Kennington the worship leader received a picture and prophecy. He saw a gathering of clergy, but instead of clerical collars, they wore collars of snakeskin, and their surplices were stained with blood. In their eyes was a look of contempt and defiance.

And the Lord said, 'See the clergy and how they are dressed! I want you to know that their garments are stained with blood, for I hold them responsible for the blood of the innocent and accountable for injustice. For they knew my words, the truth that I gave them, but they have shut their lips.

'They have made my holy name a stench in the nostrils of the unsaved. Moreover, they have spoken falsehood in my name, calling 'just' what I have not called just, and declaring innocent those I have declared guilty. Therefore I am about to remove their robes from them, and their covering from about them, so that the world will see that they are but men, and not my people.' [28]

Salt and Light in the Nation June 1992

When I formed you, I took you and I drew you out and separated you from an institution which was lost in the darkness of unbelief and false teaching. I restored to you the truth of my word, and I set you in this nation as a repository of that truth and in order that you might declare and act as guardian of that truth as it is contained in my holy word.

I appointed you in order that you might be salt and light in this nation where I have placed you; in order that through you I might bring godly wisdom and enlightenment to the rulers of this nation and the knowledge of the way of truth and upright living to its people. I inspired those who wrote your prayer book and through it I provided you with direction as to how you should uphold the nation's rulers before me.

Ever since I formed you, I have cherished you and protected you from your enemies, both within and without, in order that you might continue to be an instrument of my righteousness. Yet, despite all this, you have disregarded the sacred trust which I have given to you and you have lightly esteemed the rich inheritance which I placed into your hands.

Your leaders have despised me and have rejected my word. They have played the harlot, loving the world and the things of the world. In seeking to be pleasers of men they have discarded piece by piece the doctrines contained in my word in order that they may not give offence to men.

Instead of sounding a trumpet-call of warning to those who were turning aside after teachings which were not true, they have chosen rather to join hands with them and walk in the path of darkness, closing their eyes to those portions of my word which have become inconvenient.

Your nation has turned away from me and gone astray with the approval of the church. It has passed laws which are an offence against me, while the voices of your leaders have been either silent or sometimes heard in approval. Instead of standing as a bulwark of strength against the flood which threatens to engulf your nation and sweep it away in a tidal wave of anarchy and immorality, they have assisted those who in foolishness have opened the door to those forces of darkness.

The position of your sovereign as the upholder of the Gospel, according to the oath which she swore before me, has been compromised as a result of walking according to the counsel of her spiritual advisers, who have sacrificed godliness and truth on the altar of political and social expediency.

I have called to you many times in order that you should repent and return to walking in the ways of my word and declaring its truth to a nation lost in darkness and confusion, but you have stubbornly blocked your ears. I am deeply grieved over the state of your godless nation; but with you I am exceedingly angry on account of your faithlessness and apostasy. I warn you that unless there is speedy repentance on the part of your leaders, I will hold them accountable for the blood of many. If there is no repentance, then I will give you up to those things which you are bringing upon yourselves, and there will be no turning back. Because of your lukewarmness, I will spew you out of my mouth; because of your refusal to love the truth, I will give you up to delusion and darkness.

Even that which you still have will be lost to you. There will be division and strife and utter confusion within your own ranks. Your wealth will disappear from you and your buildings will be occupied by those who do not know me. Because of their disregard of my authority, your leaders will become a laughing stock and their pronouncements will become the subject of open ridicule by the world which for so long they have sought to please.

O, Church of England, hear the cry of my heart as I warn you, for in my anger I speak of impending judgment but in my steadfast love I plead with you, for I still love you and I still desire to bless you on account of the faithfulness of former generations.

Return to my word and obey it. Rediscover the paths of righteousness and walk in them, for if you will do so, I will even now save what little remains of your former glory and use you as an instrument of salvation in this nation; but if you do not, I will give you up to the destruction which you have chosen for yourselves, for your condition in my sight is now worse than that of the institution out of which I first rescued you. [29]

Prophecies to Britain

Clear Warnings

<u>*November 1984*</u>

God is very patient with us and sends clear warnings. But when these are ignored time after time they have the effect of breaking our relationship with him and leaving us exposed to the forces of darkness. This is what is happening in Britain and many other nations in this generation.

Specifically in regard to Britain, a prophetic word was given to a large meeting of Christians at Bath in November 1984. Part of this word, which was widely circulated, was:

'I will require the blood of this nation at the hands of my people who are not my people. Judgment will begin at the household of faith where there is no faith', says the Lord. 'Three years; I give you three years to get your house in order, or judgment will fall upon this nation and it will begin with my people who deny my word, who do not see the signs of the times, who are deaf to my words and blind to my deeds. They do not bring my word to the nation in a time of great danger.' [30]

During the following three years a number of significant warning signs were given. These came to a climax in October 1987 with the hurricane that hit London and South-East England. Forty-eight hours later, the great stock market crash shook financial capitals around the world. In London this was followed shortly after by the terrible fire in Kings Cross Underground station in which 30 people died and many were injured.

These events shook the whole nation but there was no prophetic call from church leaders interpreting the signs and declaring the word of God to the nation. In the January 1988 Editorial in Prophecy Today attention was drawn to the six sins of Jerusalem in Jeremiah chapter 7, and a comparison drawn with our own times. The Editorial stated:

The six sins of Jerusalem were – **false religion; injustice; oppression; murder; idolatry; and immorality**. Through the prophet God warned Jerusalem around the year 590 BC that unless they turned away from these sinful ways and put their trust in him he would no longer protect them from the enemy but would allow the nation of Judah and the city of Jerusalem, including the Temple, to be destroyed. God will not protect an unholy and rebellious generation who deliberately turn their their backs upon him and are deaf and blind to his word. Between 1984 and 1987 there were six major warning signs to the nation, each correlating to one of the six sins of Jerusalem.

First sign – false religion The first sign was to the church, a warning about false religion. It came with the lightning strike upon York Minster that set fire to the part of the building in which Dr David Jenkins had just been consecrated Bishop of Durham.

Second sign – idolatry The second sign was the warning about idolatry, turning from the truth to false gods. It happened in Bradford, where Britain's first Muslim Lord Mayor had just been sworn in on the Koran and in which just a few hours later the football stadium caught fire with the loss of fifty-five lives. Now let me make it abundantly clear that I am not saying that God sent this as a deliberate act of punishment – NO, NO, NO! God grieves with us in our human tragedies caused by human negligence, as was this one. But it was a *sign*. A sign in biblical language is an event with a spiritual interpretation that focuses the attention of the entire nation and through which God can convey a message to his people.

Third sign – immorality The third sign was about immorality. It was the government campaign warning of the dangers of AIDS. Its message warned against unsafe sex, recommending the use of condoms. It did not warn against sexual promiscuity, which was the message of the sign. But it is not the responsibility of government to interpret spiritual signs. That is the task of the *church!*

Fourth sign – injustice The fourth sign was a warning about injustice. It was the sinking of the cross channel ferry, The *Herald of Free Enterprise*. Again I repeat: this was not a direct act of God that resulted in the deaths of nearly two hundred people. Its immediate cause was human error. The warning was about unbridled greed and corruption in the economy that makes the acquisition of material wealth more important than the care of human life.

Fifth sign – murder The fifth sign was a warning about murder and the 'shedding of innocent blood'. It was the Hungerford massacre in which a man under satanic possession, believing he was serving a serpent god, took a machine-gun and went on a rampage of murder and mayhem through the quiet country town of Hungerford.

Sixth sign – oppression The sixth sign was oppression. It came with the hurricane that hit only the most affluent area of Britain. In biblical/Hebrew understanding, oppression means the misuse of power – the use of our positions of privilege for our own selfish ends through which we oppress those less powerful than ourselves in the family, in the community or in the nation.

God warned the people of Jerusalem what he would do unless they turned from their sinful ways, 'My anger and my wrath will be poured out on this place, on man and beast, on the trees of the field and on the fruit of the ground, and it will burn and not be quenched' (Jeremiah 7:20). In south-east England sixteen million trees were destroyed in two hours of hurricane-force winds. There was not an apple left on the fruit trees in Kent, known as the Garden of England, where they were picking the Coxes and Bramleys. The houses of the rich worth five times the value of houses in the north of England, were battered and scarred with an estimated £500m-worth of damage.

Beginning of judgment As we began to listen to early-morning news of the extent of storm damage I felt God saying that this was the sixth and final warning and that the first signs of judgment – judgment in the economy – would soon begin. Forty-eight hours later world stock markets began tumbling and London experienced the worst crash of all with millions of pounds wiped off share values. 'Hurricane Friday' was followed by 'Black Monday' in the City of London as the winds of panic swept through world financial markets. Judgment on the rich nations had begun.

I believe that the hurricane was the sixth and last of the warning signs and that we have now actually entered the beginnings of a time of judgment upon Britain. But I also believe it was a promise of revival. However, like all God's promises of blessing, it is conditional. The condition is similar to that which Solomon received and which begins 'If my people . . .' (2 Chronicles 7:14).

Looking ahead into the coming year I believe we shall see more disasters in 1988, with deepening worldwide economic problems compounded by increasing violence among the nations and, internally, social unrest and lawlessness, especially in western countries.

But it is not only the nations that are being shaken, it is also the church. Churches throughout the West are coming under judgment; in America, for the obscene materialism and vast affluence that is an offence to God; in Britain and Europe, for their unbelief and intellectual pride that deny the word of God and are a barrier to his saving power reaching the peoples. The Church of England in particular will be shaken to its core.

The word of the Lord for our times is still, 'I am shaking the nations to bring forth the Kingdom' (Hebrews 12:26-29). God is using the wickedness of mankind as well as natural forces to shake man's confidence in 'created things' so that what cannot be shaken (the Kingdom of God) may be established among the nations. Thus although we are now moving into a time of increased shaking we will also see revival and great spiritual awakening among the nations. The times of harvesting the multitudes have begun.

After October 1987 the PWM Ministry Team spent a lot of time interceding on behalf of the nation. Specifically we were asking that the period of grace might be extended and the forces of destruction held back.

We were clearly drawn to the parable of the fig-tree in Luke 13: 6-9, in which the householder went to look for fruit on the tree but did not find any: 'For three years now I have been coming to look for fruit on this fig-tree and have not found any. Cut it down!' The gardener pleaded, 'Leave it alone for one more year, and I will dig round it and fertilise it. If it bears fruit next year, fine! If not, then cut it down.'

We published this in Prophecy Today *(March/April 1988) and felt God say that he would extend the time, and that he was again calling upon the church to repent before the word would be heard in the nation. Many Christians did respond to the message and a National Day of Repentance and Prayer was held on 5 March 1988. But there was no great turning to God in either church or nation.*

The end of November 1988 arrived. Then, in December, a series of disasters began. First, the Clapham Junction railway crash in London, when a rush-hour train packed with commuters ploughed into the back of a similarly filled train. Two weeks later Pan Am Flight 103 fell from the skies onto Lockerbie, scattering wreckage and bodies over ten thousand square metres of countryside. Two-and-a-half weeks after that the nation was stunned by another airliner crash, this time onto the M1 motorway. This was followed four months later by the Sheffield Hillsborough football disaster in which 95 lives were lost, most of them young people from Liverpool.

Human Error

April 1989

One week before the Liverpool football tragedy (April 1989), we received a letter from the vicar of St John's Church Liverpool commenting on the statement in Prophecy Today that God was using the series of recent disasters as warning signs to the nation. He wrote:

I subscribe to your view that they are warnings from God but I believe I detect a noticeable addition. This is in the manner in which some of these accidents are now occurring, whereby they are not necessarily any longer "acceptable" human error or caused by circumstances beyond normal control. They are beginning to be caused by inexplicable human error.

I believe that God is using this to speak to us and that he is saying:

'The disasters I am allowing to come upon you as warnings are not being taken seriously by you. You are finding reasons to explain them away – the hurricane, the floods and the droughts as part of nature's excesses; the accidents as the work of assassins or terrorists, or the result of mechanical failure or excusable human error. So I will allow to come upon you that which you cannot explain. Your technical skill and scientific knowledge will not supply an answer to the tragedies you suffer, so that you will be forced to look in another direction – my direction – for an explanation.' [31]

Sons not Orphans

January 1986

I have not forsaken this land. Can a father so readily and easily forget his children? I have loved you, called you and received you, yet you are like my servant Israel, never resting in my provision, security and safety. O Britain, how much farther must you go upon this road of destruction and disaster, how much farther must you ride in the storm of political and social upheaval? I have spoken, beckoned you, for I would show you that my way is the only way to peace, prosperity and security.

In my Son you can have life, only turn from your wickedness unto me, and be filled with a knowledge of the Almighty, who calls you today. It is not my will to visit judgment upon you. I offer you forgiveness, grace and mercy, only turn to me with your whole heart and not with your lips alone that I may restore you and speak to the nations through you. The day of the Lord is very near, a day of power and judgment, a day of ultimate glory, for the whole earth shall know that I am the Lord. O Britain, hear and heed my call and let me visit you this day with grace and mercy and the revelation of my deep love for you, for I would call you not as orphans but as sons. [32]

Message to the City of London

January 1986

I weep over this city of London, even as I wept over Jerusalem. For as Jerusalem did not receive me or recognise my presence in her midst, so London has not received me. As the fruit of this rejection I see great wickedness coming out of this city bringing corruption and degradation to the farthest parts of the earth and I say to you that this city is ripe for destruction.

Days of judgment and tribulation shall come upon this city the like of which you have never seen or imagined, even as days of judgment and tribulation came upon Jerusalem in fulfilment of my word. In that day many will cry to me and I will say to them 'In the day when I cried to you and called to you to repent and walk in my ways, you were deaf to my cry, you rejected those whom I sent to you, so I say to you except you turn to me with mourning and with weeping and with deep repentance, I will be deaf to your cry.'

I say to many of you who call yourselves by my name, that you have honoured me with your lips but your hearts are far from me. You have served your own interests and not my Kingdom. You have become preoccupied with trivialities when I have called you to great exploits in my name, that you have turned away the wounded and crippled and the sick whom I would have had you heal, and you have served yourselves.

I say to you that in the day when I act in judgment do not imagine that my protection will surround you because you have called yourself by my name, any more than my protection was on the people of Jerusalem because my temple was in their midst.

To this one will I look, the one who is of a humble and contrite heart and who trembles at my word, but the proud and the arrogant and those who boast in their own righteousness will be as stubble to be consumed before the fire of my wrath, says the Lord. [33]

City of Mammon

September 1987

The following prophecy was given specifically for the City of London where the great dome of St Paul's Cathedral surmounted with a gold cross which used to be the highest point in the City is now dwarfed by the NatWest Bank Tower, symbol of the dominance of the great banking institutions in the City.

'Woe to the City, full of idolatry. You worship at the altar of mammon and you are steeped in greed and self-indulgence. The days will come when you will throw away your idols of silver and gold, your gods of bonds and shares, and you will cry out to the Lord for mercy. The day of the Lord comes as a thief in the night to snatch away your treasure and the great empires you have built. They are built upon sand and not upon rock.

'Woe to you who are rich but are not rich towards God. You say you have no need of anything, you can solve every problem and face any issue. You will be brought low. Your great finance houses will crumble and collapse like a house of cards.

'I will judge the harlot of Threadneedle Street and her sisters for the injustice and oppression upon which their prosperity is founded. The day of reckoning cannot be long delayed. Your cup of iniquity is full. Woe to him who trusts in the arm of flesh and does not heed the word of God. Let justice flow down like a river, like the never-ceasing Thames.' [34]

A Scorching Wind

November 1990

I am about to send a strong scorching wind upon my people, a wind that is too strong to winnow or to cleanse, a wind that will scorch and wither, will destroy and scatter. I will blow upon all that is raised up by the might of man, built in the power of the flesh. I will scorch and wither all that is sown in falsehood and deception, all that is sown in carnality, for my word is not being handled accurately as my holy unchanging word.

When that scorching wind has passed, some of the structures will still seem to stand as stalks of straw standing among the debris, but they will be lifeless and fruitless. Yet from the ground you will see new shoots appearing – green, fresh, living.

Those who have honoured my name and hold to my word, who have gathered together out of reverence for my name, I will remember; and from the destruction of that wind I will gather my bride – holy, undefiled and obedient to me.

I tell you this now so that when you see the destruction, division and lifeless structures of churches and organisations, you will know that it was I who sent the wind, but you who honour me and reverence my name will be precious in my sight. [35]

An Issachar People

<u>*May 1990*</u>

In the late 1980s and early 1990s there were widespread expectations of imminent revival that were being built up among Christians in Britain by some church leaders with more spiritual enthusiasm than discernment. There was even an expectation among some that revival would break out in the UK in the autumn of 1990, with people falling down in the streets slain in the Spirit, and miraculous healings occurring throughout the land that would be featured on TV.

My response is 'Amen, Lord. Let it happen!' But the Spirit within me declares this to be a false expectation and to warn against filling the people with false hopes through crying 'Peace, Peace' when the Lord is saying, 'There is no peace!' There will be no revival in Britain without repentance. Indeed revival will come! But it will not come until the breaking of the nation and the church. The revival will come out of the brokenness, and not before. The true word of the Lord is to prepare the people for the days of darkness that are coming, that at least the remnant may be able to withstand the testing days and to take a firm stand against deception or compromise with the truth.

This is what the Lord says to the people of Britain:

'I sent a lightning strike upon York Minster, yet you did not return to me. I sent the plague of AIDS among you, the fruit of an adulterous generation, yet you did not return to me, says the Lord. I allowed disasters to come upon you that caused much grief and sadness and caused me to grieve also, yet you did not return to me, says the Lord.

'I withheld the rain and sent a drought on some parts of the land and unseasonal weather on others, yet you did not return to me, says the Lord. I sent strange diseases upon your cattle and upon your hens and upon your factory farms that are an abomination to me, yet you did not return to me, says the Lord.

'I sent a hurricane to sweep across south-east England as a sign to you, felling great trees and causing havoc in your most prosperous area, yet you did not return to me, says the Lord. I caused the Stock Market to crash as a sign of my anger against the greed of the wealthy and the injustice done to the poor and the powerless, yet you did not return to me, says the Lord.

'I sent economic problems and hardships upon you that the wisdom of man is unable to solve, yet you have not returned to me, says the Lord. I sent storms to rage across your land to terrify even the stout-hearted as a sign of my anger, yet you have not returned to me, says the Lord.

'Surely I have been merciful in my warning signs and forbearing in my great patience. In my great love I have sent you warning after warning. But you have ignored the signs I sent to you, you have spurned my word and closed your ears to my voice.

Shall I now continue to hold back the forces of destruction that are poised to strike you, to bring judgment upon this nation that has had my word of truth for centuries and has turned its back upon me? You have chosen darkness rather than light; you shall indeed have darkness. The time is coming and now is about to break upon you when you will long for the light and you will cry out for the day. But you will not see the light until the forces of darkness have accomplished their work. Night is coming, but also the day' (see Amos 4:6-12). [36]

A Word to the Nation based on Deut: 28: 16-37

<u>May 1992</u>

This is what the Lord says, Unless you repent and turn to me –

[16] Disasters will occur in your cities and in the countryside. [17] Inflation will continue to curse the economy. [18] An increasing number of babies will be conceived with incurable diseases. The crops of your land will be blighted and strange, unknown animal diseases will afflict your flocks and herds. [19] You will have no peace on your borders. Your international relationships will always be difficult. There will be growing unease and mistrust among the surrounding nations as international tension increases throughout the world.

[20] Confusion will mark all your political programmes, your social reforms and your economic policies until you learn the meaning of 'not by might, nor by power, but by my word, says the Lord.'* [21] You will see plagues and unknown diseases afflict your people. [22] You will see AIDS claiming the lives of great numbers and striking terror into the whole population. [23] Drought and blight and crop diseases will devastate the countryside and reduce your harvests, which will further weaken the economy and threaten famine among the people. [24] Acid rain will descend upon you and pollution will contaminate the land, the water, and the air you breathe.

[25] Terrorist groups will arise to strike fear into great nations, and you will live under threat from those who see you as their enemies. [27] New diseases will come upon you that even the advances in medical science will not be able to cure. [28] The mental health of the nation will deteriorate sharply. Your psychiatric units and hospitals will not be able to cope with the confusion and madness that will afflict the population. [29] Great depression will come upon the people, a sense of hopelessness and despair, that will lead many to suicide. [30] There will be great breakdown of marriage and family life, and rape and violence will become common in the community.

[31] Bankruptcy will plague business life and home repossessions will bring grief and suffering to many people. [32] Child abuse will become commonplace and even child slavery will occur, and you will be powerless to stop the exploitation of your little ones. [33] Aliens will become increasingly powerful in your land. They will even force you to worship their gods which they will establish in your land. [35] The health of the whole nation will suffer, from the oldest to the youngest, the rich and the poor, the rulers and the people. [36] Your own government will be powerless to protect you and you will be ruled from outside your land. Others will make the laws that govern you, and you will be oppressed and afflicted and become an object of scorn and ridicule to all the nations.

* I am aware that Zechariah 4:6 says '. . . by my Spirit', but this is what was received, possibly because the 'word' is for the nation but the 'Spirit' for the church. [37]

Scotland ... God Speaks to a Nation

<u>*April 1985*</u>

On 20 April 1985, many Christians from all over Scotland gathered in Edinburgh for a day of 'repentance and intercession' for the nation. This plan was born in prayer by an intercessor, Jean Black, who was the coordinator for 'Lydia Fellowship' in Scotland. Christians assembled and marched up Princes Street to Calton Hill, which overlooks this beautiful capital of Scotland.

There they worshipped God, who is the Governor over the nations, and cried to him for a moving of his spirit throughout the land. Then they assembled in the Church of Scotland Assembly room, outside of which there is a monument to John Knox who cried, 'give me Scotland or I die'.

There they worshipped God, and humbled themselves, and interceded for the nation. During the word which was preached, the following prophetic utterance was given.

O Scotland, Scotland, land of hills and valleys, how oft would I have gathered you together as a hen doth gather her young under her wings, but you would not. You are a nation that has forgotten its God, and turned from the faith of your fathers. Yet I have shown you my grace and my mercy, and still you have turned your backs. You have despised my holy law, and have not by prayer and precept taught your children the knowledge of the creator, and the way he can be known, through the only saviour, Jesus Christ.

How I would have delighted to exalt you, but you have turned from righteousness, and it is righteousness which exalteth a nation, but sin is a reproach to any people. You have chosen your own ways, therefore there is a blight on the land ... a blight of poverty, of lawlessness ... a blight of unhappiness, and a blight of hopelessness. And yet if you would turn to me with all your heart, and turn to righteousness, by turning from sin, and receiving my son, Jesus, I would yet exalt you again.

Many shepherds have scattered my flock, and thus proved that they are hirelings. The sick they have not visited ... the lost they have not sought, and yet they have gone in the guise of leaders of my people.

Woe to those who have not cared.
Woe to those who have not sought my face.
Woe to those who have not diligently taught my word.
Woe to those who have preached another gospel.
Woe to those who have denied my word.

Yet I am a God of mercy, and long-suffering, forgiving, and when there is true repentance for your sins and your hypocrises, then there will be true forgiveness. I am slow to anger and swift to bless.

Still I call my people, that if they will humble themselves and pray, and seek my face, and turn from their wicked ways, I will bring healing to the land.

I will bring hope where there is hopelessness.
I will bring joy where there is sadness.
I will bring healing where there is sickness.
I will bring strength where there is weakness.
I will bring plenty where there is poverty, because the righteous are never forsaken, nor do their seed beg bread.
I will bring unity where there is division.
I will bring salvation where there is sin.
I will bring fruitfulness where there is barrenness.

My church shall be a light, and a blessing in the midst of the land, and manifest my life, my love, and power, when my people walk in my ways, and truly love one another.

I greatly desire to bless. Did I not already show you as a nation, in Lewis, what I can do when I pour out my Spirit, I desire to do so again, but in a way that you would not think possible, for I will do a new thing. If you will ... I will.

But if not ... the land will be left to you desolate. Desolate of hope. The oil will cease to flow, and the land will not yield the same increase. Must I send judgment before you will harken to my voice? I delight in mercy ... turn ye, turn ye, why will you die?

On this day I speak to this nation. Note this day well. I do hear from heaven ... I do acknowledge repentance ... I do forgive sin, but rend your hearts, and not your garments, that I may pour a blessing upon you.

The blessing of the outpouring of my spirit on a thirsty land.

The blessing of revelation of myself.

The blessing of peace and joy.

The blessing of being like a watered garden whose waters fail not, that the nation might see the manifestation of divine favour on a people who have chosen to obey my voice, love, and serve me.

Then will flow the blessing of the Lord which maketh rich, not only on her own land, but from your land to others.
If my people will, I will ... if you will, I will. [38]

International Prophecies

Prophecy to the Nations of Europe

<u>March 1985</u>

The Word of God for our Times

This is what the Lord says to Europe. If only you had paid attention to my word you would have enjoyed peace in your time. You have had the word of life for many centuries, yet you have not heeded it! You have followed your own ways and not sought my way. Therefore you have been led astray by men of violence. Therefore you have been ravished by the enemy. You have seen your cities torn asunder, the flower of your youth cut down, men in the prime of life taken from you, because you have not sought my way.

I am watching! I the Lord, neither slumber nor sleep, and I will avenge those who suffer at the hands of evil men. I hate the corruption of the innocent. I cannot tolerate the exploitation of the poor and the powerless by unscrupulous men.

The men of violence will be brought to judgment. The men with blood on their hands who fight worthless causes in the name of freedom and who proclaim liberty but by their actions destroy the very thing they proclaim, they shall be revealed for the evil of their hearts.

Take heed now you Europeans who have seen a century of strife, you shall see more. The day of the Lord is at hand! It is a day of darkness and not of light. It is a day when the evil in the hands of men will be revealed. They are afraid to come to the light lest their deeds be seen for what they are. But the Light is coming to you O Europe, and that coming will be a day of judgment upon your evil and rebellious generation.

Everywhere I look I see injustice and lies. I do not see men of truth. They speak smooth things with their tongues, but evil in their hearts. Each man cares only for himself and not for his neighbour. Therefore strife and discord is in every community, and disunity reigns among the nations of Europe.

Yet I love you and I plead with you to turn to me and be saved; to seek my way and live. I do not wish to see destruction come upon you. You are special to me. I have loved you through the centuries and you have done much to carry the Gospel throughout the world. Why have you turned away from me? Who has bewitched you? Why have you forsaken my word and devised your own philosophies that do not take account of my word, or my ways, and that defy my law? You are a rebellious people who cannot claim ignorance of my requirements. You know my word and yet you have turned your back upon me.

Because you are a rebellious people and have turned away from my word and have not walked in my way, nor sought my will, I will bring judgment upon you. Woe to you who are rich! You will be brought low. You who have grown fat and sleek on the profits you have made from exploiting the poor, you shall be humbled. You who boast of your great international corporations, lo your houses will be left to you, desolate. You who purvey filth and violence, who degrade your humanity to satisfy your lustful desires. Consider now the consequences of your actions. See where they have led you. Look back at your history since the 'Great Enlightenment'. The Great Enlightenment is the great illusion! It has blinded the minds of men to the reality of truth. The truth is hidden from them. Well may it be said of this generation, 'They have eyes but they do not see, they have ears but they do not hear, they have minds but they do not think, they have hearts but they do not love, – except to love themselves'.

This is a self-seeking generation. The enemy has blinded their eyes so that they cannot perceive the simple realities of life. They will go into the pit like the Gadarene swine following their own leaders without thought and without care. They care for neither man nor God. They do not pause to think or stop to reflect on the path they have trodden, or the path they are following – where it leads. It is the way of death and destruction.

Turn to me and be saved O nations of Europe. For I am God and there is no other. I created the universe and set the stars in their orbits. I created man in my own image and I love my creation. I the Lord declare my love for you, my rebellious children. Once more I plead with you as a father pleads with his wayward child. [39]

To the Leaders of South Africa

November 1985

Sent to the Prime Minister and Government of South Africa through a Christian minister friend of the Prime Minister

Thus says the Lord to the leaders of South Africa.

How dare you misuse my word to support your own evil prejudices and obnoxious system of economic slavery and oppression! It is utterly abhorrent to me.

The day will come when the black men will wreak a savage revenge upon you. I do not desire the slaughter that is coming upon you. I desire your repentance and not your death. I seek justice and mercy, not violence and murder.

Repent now and turn away from your evil ways and seek my way. Establish justice in the land before the sword of Damocles falls upon you. The day of reckoning is not far off. Repent now that you may live and live in peace. [40]

International Prophecies

To the Leaders of the Soviet Union

April 1986

Given at the 'Jerusalem Gathering' April 1986, three weeks before the Chernobyl nuclear powerstation blew up, which began the sequence of events leading to the collapse of the Soviet Union

'For many years you have denied me. You have persecuted my people and brought shame on the name of Russia. You have become a byword among the nations for oppression. You who sought freedom and justice for all have become the most monstrous persecutors and oppressors of all time.

'Woe to you, leaders of the people! Woe to you who oppress those who seek freedom and who attempt to speak in the name of Justice. You will suffer a harsher judgment than you pass on those you oppress. You who spend the money you grind from the poor and exact from the powerless to build your mighty armies, you will unleash the floodtide of vengeance that shall consume all around you and bring down your evil regime.

'The Kremlin shall crumble. The edifice of Lenin will be erased from the land. Men will spit upon you and see your humiliation, because you have made yourselves gods and scorned my word and set yourself against me.

'You cannot stand in the day that I come. That day will not be long delayed.' [41]

The Mother Barbara Prophecy 1911

September 1986

In 1918, shortly before Mother Barbara went to live in the community house near the Garden of Gethsemane on the Mount of Olives in Jerusalem, she was given a prophecy by Bishop Aristocoli of the Russian Orthodox Church.

Some of the events foreseen in this remarkable prophecy have already been fulfilled. The rise and fall of communism in Russia has taken place. Germany was divided in two for nearly fifty years from 1945. Britain has lost her empire and her colonies. This must have seemed almost impossible back in 1911 before the First World War when Britain ruled the largest Empire the world had ever known and was the richest and most powerful nation.

The prophecy was published in Prophecy Today *in September 1986, soon after the Carmel Gathering, where it was prophesised that the Soviet Union was about to fall. The storm clouds were already gathering over the USSR.*

'Tell the women they must belong absolutely to God. They must believe in the great things that are happening and that God is doing on the earth. They must prepare their souls, their children and their husbands. And they will have very much work to do for God. Oh, what a great work the women will have to do in the end time, and the men will follow them.

Not one country will be without trial - do not be frightened of anything you will hear. An evil will shortly take Russia and wherever this evil comes, rivers of blood will flow. This evil will take the whole world and wherever it goes, rivers of blood will flow because of it. It is not the Russian soul, but an imposition on the Russian soul. It is not an ideology, or a philosophy, but a spirit from hell. In the last days Germany will be divided in two. France will just be nothing. Italy will be judged by natural disasters. Britain will lose her empire and all her colonies and will come to almost total ruin, but will be saved by praying women. America will feed the world, but will finally collapse. Russia and China will destroy each other. Finally, Russia will be free and from her, believers will go forth and turn many from the nations to God.'

Sound the Alarm – Nigeria

<u>*November 1987*</u>

The violent persecution that is accompanying revival in Nigeria is seen by Christian leaders there as part of the plan of the enemy to try to disrupt the work of God and stop the preaching of the Gospel. In a message sent out to 'Prayer for the Nation' groups throughout Nigeria a powerful plea was made for Christians to pray and enter into spiritual warfare. The statement said:

'We challenge believers not to cringe and cower. The time for us to be courageous is now. God has not given us the spirit of fear, but of love, of power and of a sound mind. Our God emboldens us, for he said we shall be made willing in the days of his power. Such days are here with us. Chins up, brethren, God is on our side! We encourage you to pursue relentlessly the business of personal evangelism. We must preach the Gospel on a one-to-one basis. Evangelism is a powerful weapon of Christian warfare. Let us be strong in the Lord and in the power of his might. Let us put on the whole armour of God that we may be able to stand against the wiles of the devil!'

The above message was accompanied by the following prophecy:

'You will blow the trumpet. You will sound an alarm in the camps of my people and you will say to them, "This is the battle that I have spoken about in times past." Tell them you are moving close to the battle. You shall say unto them, "Prepare yourself, for it is a battle of destiny that will determine not only the destiny of your country but of Africa." Tell them that the city shall be possessed, but not without a price. Tell them to put on the armour of light, of prayer and courage. It is a holy battle.

'You must take instruction from me. Say nothing except what I give you. Tell my people to get ready for battle. For mighty trees shall fall, mighty rocks shall break and mighty mountains shall move. Do not be afraid of the darkness, for darkness shall come. But it is in the midst of darkness that the light shines brighter. The light is more than darkness, for it has strength to overcome darkness. The Lord will utter his voice before his people and the camp of the Lord shall be great.' [42]

Time of Trial

January 1988

'Thus says the Lord, I am about to shake the earth, to shake the nations, and to sift you as wheat is sifted. I will separate the chaff from the wheat.

'As I did in the land of Egypt so will I do with you. I will make a difference between those who are my people and those who belong to the gods of this world.

'Turn to me with all your heart and put away your idols from among you; deal righteously and justly in all that you do, for you are mine, and my name which is holy shall be honoured and uplifted among you.

'I am about to bring a time of great trial upon the world, but you who obey me will know my favour and my protection. There will be weeping and wailing and great distress all around you, but your needs will be supplied when all the systems of this world fail. All people will see that I care for you, but only as you obey me and sanctify me in your hearts.' [43]

Turn Again to Me, My People

<u>March 1989</u>

'I gave you the world and asked you to shape it and lead it in thanksgiving and praise of my goodness and glory. I gave you my son, my only son, to show you once more how to do my will in the world. What more can I give you, my people? What more can I do to bring you to the narrow path that leads to salvation?

'The time is coming soon when I will bring justice on earth, and that will mean a great and painful rearrangement of the way that the earth's resources are used. You have piled up riches in one place and left nothing in another; you have used the good things of the world selfishly and denied them to those in need; you have sowed suspicion and fear among the peoples and sold them weapons of destruction and oppression to give them power over their neighbours; you have turned my creation away from my purposes and used it to give yourselves comfort and idleness.

'My children, you are not gods. You see only the surface of things, the immediate result of your actions. The walls you have built around yourselves are made only of straw. They prevent you seeing what is happening outside but they give you no protection. When they are broken down you will still be unprepared and defenceless.

'Your wealth and comfort is an offence to the poor. When they rise against you, who will defend you? Your medicines and science prolong your lives but leave you unprotected when some new disease strikes you. Who will heal you then?

'My creation is not mocked; you cannot isolate yourselves from it. One day the world will break into your cocoon and you will have no resistance to offer.

'Turn again to me. Share your riches with the poor. Accept your place among my servants and do not pretend to be gods. There is still time, but it is very short. I do not want you to suffer but I cannot delay my justice much longer and your situation is very near to disaster. Turn back to me and put all your trust in me; I will protect you, says the Lord.' [44]

Out of the Mouths of Children

<u>March 1990</u>

'Those who listen will be the ones who are called. For I will fill the mouths of little children with exhortations which can come only from divine revelation. They will be given divine utterance in order to build one another up and swell the kingdom of God.

'Across the world children will be brought to the foot of the cross, past agonies will be lifted from them, as they first seek the kingdom of God.

'They will be a mighty force, for they come in their naivete. Under the anointing of the Holy Spirit they will minister to young and old.

'Listen to me. Discern the gravity of the times. Do not impede their walk by cossetting them, and do not apprehend the work of the Spirit.

'I will meet them on the hills, in the valleys and forests and on the plains. Neither ghetto nor palace will be able to hold back the work of the Spirit in their lives.

'Those who live in the outermost parts of the world will be given sublime visions that no man could have foretold. Others will speak with angels, others will be transported in the Spirit, where they will testify to the sovereign power of their Lord Jesus Christ.

'Such will be the anointing upon them that they will step on minefields and not be hurt, their bellies will be empty and they will not be hungry, they will go without sleep and not be tired, for they will be given the ability and strength to overcome.' [45]

The Overcomers

<u>*November 1990*</u>

The Lord says, 'Look to Eastern Europe and learn. They have learned to persevere under trial. They know what it is to follow Jesus and go the way of the cross. They know what it is to endure with joy because of the hope to which they have been called. They know what it is to see the light shine in the darkness. They are overcomers. Great is their reward, great is their love. Great is their faithfulness, and it will not be taken away from them.

'Do not corrupt them with materialistic idolatry and vain imaginations. For though in your eyes they are poor – yet they are rich. There is great victory in suffering so do not be blinded by worldly thinking. They have endured much and learned much – listen to them, for you in the West will need their wisdom and support as you learn to persevere under trial.

'You look to your technology and material wealth as a sign of maturity; this is pride. This is immaturity. I do not need fancy gadgets and wealth to proclaim the honour of my name.

'No! What I am looking for is a humble heart, a contrite spirit, a people who are obedient, willing to learn, willing to listen, willing to care. Learn these things from your brothers and sisters in the East. Then you will be pure, humble, full of love and persevering as they are.' [46]

Choose Today whom you will Serve!

November 1997

The world system is creaking at the seams – it will break up and end – bringing unhappiness and turmoil. Some of my people speak of revival and peace – but no peace can come upon a world and a system, which is godless and corrupt, which owes no allegiance to the Prince of Peace. Do not be deceived, for even the lull in the middle of a storm, in the midst of bad weather, does not signal the end of the storm.

Revival may bring a lull in the storm, but the storm gathers force to break again with unrelenting violence. The strong storm clouds already fill the horizon and these darken the ends of the earth. Some look up in fear, and try to escape the storm – but there is no hiding place. The anger of dark forces will make the blood of my people flow. It is time to count the cost.

The defence of man's pride will be broken – the pride of life, the trust in the power of wealth and position will not save. It will come, the storm will come. Do you not already hear the howling of the wind, and the darkening of the skies to bring near the time of judgment of nations, and of peoples, both great and small? Some of my people will be taken, but some will remain in the hour of judgment, when light and darkness meet for final contest over the souls of men.

Therefore, decide today whom you will serve – your very souls depend on this decision. Choose life, beyond life, even through the blood of sacrifice, if needs be. [47]

You have forgotten me

June 1998

You have set the children's teeth on edge. You have taken from them the innocence I gave them when I entrusted them to you. You have deprived the children of their bread – their right to know my laws, to have them inscribed on their hearts.

Your own hearts are far from me and you have forgotten me. In the West you have set up the idols of commerce and greed, and your children are practised in the arts of self-advancement. You depend on Mammon for your security: you ignore the poor and the destitute. In your confusion you turn to pagan beliefs and old superstitions in pursuit of happiness and success but all these blessings will elude you. You work seven days in the week and you will experience the effects of your own madness in stress and disease.

Many children whose families are breaking up will not forgive you in years to come. Their hearts will be hardened, their spirits full of revenge for the childhood that was ravished from them. They will turn against you and against one another: there will be no more loyalty, but only betrayal, with every man for himself. There will be loneliness and despair on a scale never seen before, and the heavens will be as brass.

Only a remnant who are faithful to me will be saved. They will be ridiculed and mocked for their allegiance to me, but I will never forsake them. They will be oppressed and they will suffer on account of the rising tide of lawlessness.

My word will judge the nations and those who reject and abuse me.

The British people have cast me aside and it will confound them. Only repent, and my love will restore and rebuild you. [48]

Index

Index

Introduction — 3

Prophecies to the Church

1	Sound the Trumpet Shirly Archer given at Tunbridge Wells Christian Fellowship	Nov 1984	8
2	If My People Clifford Hill given at a PWM Trustees' meeting	May 1985	9
3	The Way of the Cross Clifford Hill given at a service in East London	Nov 1985	9
4	Tears of Joy Pat Rosamund, South Shields, Tyne and Wear	Jan 1986	10
5	Receive from my Hand ... Jim Graham, Minister, Gold Hill Baptist Church	Mar 1986	11
6	A Word of Warning Roger Jameson, Marlow, Buckinghamshire	Jan 1986	12
7	Times of Refreshing David Noakes, at a PWM meeting	Mar 1986	12
8	Follow Me Barbara Fenney	Oct 1986	13
9	Repentance and Revival David Noakes in Westminster Central Hall	Mar 1988	14
10	The King is Calling Shirley Archer, Tunbridge Wells	May 1988	15
11	Church Responsible for the Nation Chifford Hill in Westminster Central Hall	Mar 1988	16
12	Repent and Return Pat Hughes, Intercessors for Britain	May 1989	17
13	Humble Yourselves David Noakes at a PWM Team Meeting	May 1989	18
14	When will you put Me First? David Noakes at a PWM Team Meeting	Jul 1989	19
15	Love and Preferment Robert Weston, Ludlow Pentecostal Church	Nov 1990	20
16	New Life in Christ Clifford Hill at a PWM Team Meeting	Jul 1994	21

Index

17	Removing the Boundary Stones Alex Buchanan at Spring Harvest	Apr 1994	21
18	Walking on Water David Noakes at a PWM Team Meeting	Nov 1994	23
19	A Call to Holiness Lorna White	Jan 1995	25
20	Grieving the Heart of God Carol Weir, Hampshire	Jan 1997	26
21	I Will Keep you Safe A 13 year old girl at a summer camp near Edinburgh	Mar 1990	28
22	Consecrated Children A 14 year old boy at a summer camp near Edinburgh	Mar 1990	28
23	Miracles and Prayer A 13 year old girl at Kings Kids camp, Scotland	Jan 1991	29

Prophecies to the Church of England

24	Divine Healing Needed Clifford Hill in Southwark Cathereral	May 1984	31
25	You have been Robbed of your Power Jim Smith of the Church of England Pastoral Aid Society and read to the Conference by Bishop Colin Buchanan	April 1988	32
26	A Time to Reap Clifford Hill in Durham	Nov 1988	33
27	A Call to Repent Clifford Hill in Westminster Central Hall	Mar 1988	34
28	I Hold you Responsible Malcolm Banham in St Mark's Kennington, London	Jul 1989	34
29	Salt and Light in the Nation David Noakes	June 1992	35

Prophecies to Britain

30	Clear Warnings Clifford Hill in The Pavillion, Bath, Somerset	Nov 1984	38
31	Human Error Patrick Sykes, Vicar St John's Liverpool	Apr 1989	41
32	Sons not Orphans John Cressey, Camberwell, London	Jan 1986	42

33	Message to the City of London Tony Pearce, leader of Messianic Testimony	Jan 1986	42
34	City of Mammon Clifford Hill, PWM Team meeting	Sep 1987	43
35	A Scorching Wind Ray Borlase, leader of Intercessors for Britain	Nov 1990	44
36	An Issachar People Clifford Hill, Prophecy Today Editorial	May 1990	45
37	A Word to the Nation based on Deut: 28: 16-37 Clifford Hill, PWM Team Meeting	May 1992	47
38	Scotland ... God Speaks to a Nation Campbell McAlpine in Edinburgh, Scotland	Apr 1985	48

International Prophecies

39	Prophecy to the Nations of Europe Clifford Hill given at a Good Friday service in St Mark's Kennington, London	Mar 1985	51
40	To the Leaders of South Africa Clifford Hill at a PWM Team Meeting	Nov 1985	52
41	To the Leaders of the Soviet Union Clifford Hill in Jerusalem	Apr 1986	53
42	Sound the Alarm – Nigeria Emile Nwankpa accompanying Call to Prayer in Nigeria	Nov 1987	54
43	Time of Trial Joan Gordon-Farleigh, Harrogate, Yorkshire	Jan 1988	55
44	Turn Again to Me, My People Richard Hobbs, Newbury, Berkshire	Mar 1989	56
45	Out of the Mouths of Children Shelia Irving, Tunbridge Wells	Mar 1990	57
46	The Overcomers Heidi Lambert, in St Mark's Kennington, London	Nov 1990	58
47	Choose Today whom you will Serve! Duncan McPhee, given in St John and St Peter Parish Church, Notting Hill, London	Nov 1997	59
48	You have Forgotten Me Graham Blyth, Rector of St John the Baptist Church, Danbury, Essex	Jun 1998	60

Index 61